THE
Archive Photographs
SERIES

COBHAM
THE FLYING YEARS

To James,
With best wishes

Gordon   5/98.

Alan Cobham flies along the Thames following his return from Australia, 1 October 1926.

THE
Archive Photographs
SERIES

COBHAM
THE FLYING YEARS

Compiled by
Colin Cruddas

CHALFORD

The Chalford Publishing Company
St Mary's Mill, Chalford,
Stroud, Gloucestershire, GL6 8NX

ISBN 0 7524 0781 3

Typesetting and origination by
The Chalford Publishing Company
Printed in Great Britain by
Bailey Print, Dursley, Gloucestershire

Cover illustration: the Short Valetta used by Sir Alan Cobham on his 1931 aerial survey of central Africa under construction at Rochester.

Acknowledgments

At the SBAC Exhibition in 1966, fellow authors Mike Stroud and Derek James suggested to me that a book on Cobham, rather akin to the Dowty volume, would sit well in the Archive Photographs Series. I am indebted therefore to those gentlemen for their foresight and also to Cobham's Chief Executive, Gordon Page, for his agreement to allow me unrestricted access to the Cobham archives in order to produce this story.

The Royal Air Force Museum (Charles Brown Collection) and Hunting Aerofilms Ltd also deserve my sincere thanks with regard to photographic copyright, as do Richard Riding, Mike Hooks, Harry Holmes, Barry Abraham, Roy Brown, Frank Hambry, Peter Jolly and Rick Brewell for providing answers to my many queries and for the use of photographs from their own collections.

I am perpetually amazed that my wife Thelma can, with a light but sure touch improve upon my text - but this she does unfailingly and to great effect. For this and her proof reading skills I am deeply grateful. The word processing task would have tried the patience of a saint, but not that of Christine and Mike West who have, without a word of complaint, done a marvellous job of producing the printed page. My thanks go to them and finally, to David Buxton and the staff of the Chalford Publishing Company for their encouragement and highly professional guidance.

Contents

Acknowledgements   4

Introduction   7

1.   Early Days   9

2.   A Flying Start   15

3.   Far Away Places   29

4.   Cobham Comes to Town   59

5.   The Vital Link   77

6.   On the Lighter Side   115

7.   Flying into the Future   124

Residing today in London's National Portrait Gallery, this well known painting by artist Frank Salisbury was completed after Alan Cobham's epic flights to and from Australia in 1926.

Introduction

Many famous names are woven into the rich tapestry that forms nearly a century of British aviation. A.V. Roe, Blackburn, Fairey, Handley Page, Sopwith and de Havilland are among the best remembered examples of men who, possessing a technical qualification or disposition, themselves experimented with flying before going on to create successful aircraft manufacturing companies. Many others too achieved transient glory (or notoriety) in pitting their wits and courage against the ceaseless challenge of the skies, but this evolutionary period produced one man who became an international household name in the inter-war years. He attained a wider, more enduring fame as pioneer aviator, aerial showman, entrepreneur and visionary, founding the company that became the cornerstone of an international group which today, still bearing his marque, serves the aerospace, defence and communication industries. That man was Sir Alan Cobham.

It is hoped that these pages, which concentrate principally on his flying exploits and activities and the companies formed in his wake, will validate his claim to have been the individual most influential in furthering the cause of British civil aviation.

Sir Alan Cobham was elected master of the Guild of Air Pilots and Navigators in December 1964.

One

Early Days

Born on 6 May 1894 to Frederick and Elizabeth Cobham, young Alan John, educated at Wilson's Grammar School, Streatham, began his working life with a firm of clothing wholesalers in the City, but a subsequent brief exposure to farm work led to his joining the Army's Veterinary Corps at the outbreak of the First World War.

As the war progressed, Cobham began to recognise the importance of mechanical transport and in 1917, and by then a Staff Sergeant, he secured a transfer to the Royal Flying Corps. He completed his training in August 1918, became a commissioned instructor in what was by then the Royal Air Force and on 1 January 1919, was a civilian once again!

This reflective study shows Alan Cobham's parents and Aunt Kate (right).

Though not destined for a nautical career, young Cobham exhibited a touch of naval flair at the turn of the century.

Cobham at twelve years of age with his younger sister Vera, in 1906.

Facing a career in the ladies' lingerie business.

Volunteering for service in August 1914, Private Cobham immediately found himself on active duty in France.

Staff Sergeant Cobham was soon in charge of some 1,500 sick horses.

Smiling at last! Cobham became a flying instructor in the Royal Air Force in August 1918.

Two

A Flying Start

Determined to secure a post-war career in aviation, Cobham joined the British Aerial Transport Company. This promising start was however, short-lived, and very soon afterwards he combined forces with Fred and Jack Holmes to form the Berkshire Aviation Company. During the latter half of 1919 and the early months of 1920, Cobham toured England and Scotland giving joy-rides in a war surplus Avro 504K, and it was during this period that he met his future wife, an attractive actress who was at that time appearing at the Middlesborough Theatre.

Although the Berkshire Aviation Company continued in business for some time, a deteriorating financial situation led to Cobham withdrawing his interests and he moved to George Holt Thomas' Airco Manufacturing Company (Airco) at Hendon, where he rapidly gained valuable experience as an aerial photographic pilot. However, due to the rapid run down of the aircraft industry in the immediate post-war period, the Airco factory was forced to close not long afterwards, leaving Cobham once again seeking employment. Fortunately for him, on 1 January 1921, Geoffrey de Havilland who, throughout the war years had been Airco's Chief Designer, engaged him as the first pilot for his newly formed de Havilland Aeroplane Hire Service. In support of his new company's proud claim to 'Fly Anyone - Anywhere', Cobham now rarely seemed to be out of the cockpit; however he did, between newspaper assignments in 1922, just manage to find the time to tie the wedding knot. Routine photographic work, mainly for Aerofilms Ltd, was supplemented by air taxi and charter flying that included long distance journeys throughout Europe and the Middle East and, within a year, Cobham, now de Havilland's senior pilot, had been joined by thirteen others, including such famous personalities as Hubert Broad and Bill Hatchett. His duties embraced the test flying of new types and entering them in performance competitions both at home and abroad.

One of these was the D.H.50 in which, flying the prototype G-EBFN, he won the 1924 King's Cup Air Race at an average speed of 107mph, for which achievement he received the Royal Aero Club's Gold Medal and, for the second year running, the coveted Britannia Trophy.

Cobham's first civilian flying assignment - to find suitable landing grounds for the British Aerial Transport Company - lasted only one month. Shown here is one of the nine BAT Bantams designed and built by the Willesden-based firm.

Founder members of the Berkshire Aviation Company; from left to right: Jack Holmes, Alan Cobham, Fred Holmes and R. Graham-Wollard.

A photograph which must have graced several family albums. Nine lucky readers of the *Nottingham Evening News* won flights with Cobham in 1919.

This Avro 504K's fuselage shows signs of wear and tear that would have caused today's authorities some consternation.

COBHAM & HOLMES AVIATION Co.
(Late Berkshire Aviation Co.)

FLY WITH ALAN COBHAM

(Assisted by O. P. JONES),
THE PILOT WHO HAS CARRIED MORE PASSENGERS THAN ANY OTHER LIVING MAN.

FLYING AT WALTON BRIDGE
PRESTON,

From MARCH 1st till 14th, inclusive. 10-30 till dusk.

FLIGHTS from 21s., BOOKED AT Messrs. J. Norwood and Sons, Fishergate, Preston.

Admission to Ground 8d. (including tax).

6,000 Passengers carried this Season.

By 1920, the joy-riding operation had personalised its advertising.

Cobham was instantly captivated by Miss Gladys Lloyd, the beautiful young leading lady in the *Joy Bells* touring revue. He conducted a whirlwind courtship and within a week of their first meeting had secured her promise of marriage.

18

By mid 1920, Cobham and a photographer named McLennan had formed Airco's aerial photography department. Flying D.H.9s from the Airco site shown here, straddling the Edgware Road at Hendon, they quickly became leading exponents of the art.

Airco's photographic tasks were many and varied. Prior to 1924 when the FA Cup Final was staged at Wembley for the first time, such events often took place at Stamford Bridge, home to Chelsea FC. It is thought that this picture, taken for a national newspaper, shows Huddersfield Town and Bristol City engaged in the FA Cup Semi-final in 1920, which the northerners won 2-1.

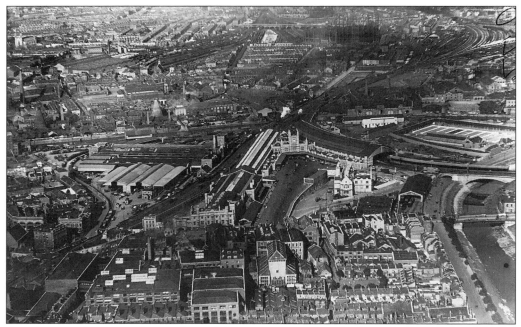

Aerial views of towns and cities formed the main part of Airco's photographic business. Shown here is the imposing approach to Bristol's Temple Meads railway station.

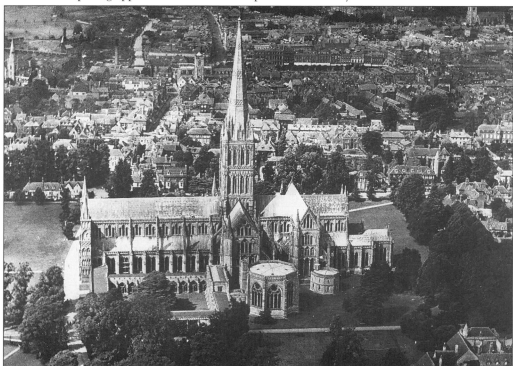

Typical of the high quality photographs produced by Airco is this fine 1920 study of Salisbury Cathedral.

Upon Airco's closure, its aerial photography interests were absorbed into Aerofilms Limited, formed in 1919 by F.L. Wills, on the left.

Cobham flew this D.H.53 *Humming Bird* from Lympne to Brussels for the 1923 Aero and Automobile Exhibition. The aircraft, powered only by a 697cc motor cycle engine, was unable to overcome moderate headwinds and had to complete the return journey by sea.

The world's first long distance charter flight took place in 1921 when Cobham flew wealthy American Lucien Sharpe around Europe and the Middle East in a D.H.9c. The journey came to an ignoble and unscheduled end when engine failure brought the aircraft down in the main shipping channel into Venice.

Cobham and Lucien Sharpe on top of Athen's 'Ancient Rock'.

St Giles' church, Bloomsbury, 30 June 1922, and the start of almost forty years of marriage. On a flying honeymoon the couple made the first airline flight between Lympne and Ostend.

In 1921 Alan Cobham was instrumental in setting up the Spanish Air Transport Company equipped with three D.H.9c aircraft.

The King's Cup Round Britain Air Race, 1923. Cobham, flying a D.H.9 powered by a Napier Lion engine, finished in second place. The aircraft was entered by vaudeville star George Robey, shown here on the steps with his wife, son-in-law and daughter Eileen, after whom the aircraft was named.

George Robey in more familiar stage attire.

King's Cup Air Race, 1924. Alan Cobham won the event on his third attempt.

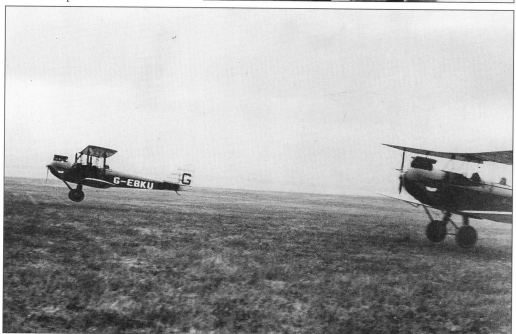

Shown here taking off in a pair of D.H. Moths, both Geoffrey de Havilland and Alan Cobham failed to complete the course in the 1925 King's Cup Air Race.

The King's Cup Air Race started and finished at Hendon aerodrome.

Two aircraft that are forever associated with Alan Cobham: the D.H.50 and, in the background, the D.H.53.

Cobham's cameraman recorded the 1921 unveiling ceremony of the memorial at Calais, dedicated to the British and French members of the Dover Patrol who lost their lives during the First World War. A British counterpart is erected on the cliffs at Dover.

Flying low over the Grand Fleet, Cobham captured the atmosphere during the Royal Review at Spithead on 26 July 1924. In the top picture the Royal Yacht, *Victoria and Albert III*, steams majestically between the assembled warships and in the lower picture, the Royal Marines complement on board the battleship *HMS Queen Elizabeth* stand ready to come to attention.

Three
Far Away Places

1924 was a momentous year for Cobham. In addition to establishing himself alongside other famous racing aviators of the day, he was chosen to accompany the Director of Civil Aviation Sir Sefton Brancker to India and Burma. The purpose of the visit was to determine the viability of setting up airship routes to the Far East, but following his safe return home (despite the odd forced landing) Brancker expressed his conviction that it would be the aeroplane and not the airship that would eventually win the day. Brancker's prophecy soon proved correct for the Imperial Airways Cairo-Baghdad-Karachi service began in 1927, three years before his untimely death in the R101 airship disaster. The return journey to India, completed in March 1925, was undertaken in D.H.50 G-EBFO, equipped with a 240 hp Puma engine, and it was this aircraft, re-equipped with a 385 hp Jaguar engine, that Cobham used later that year to fly to Cape Town.

Long distance flying was now in Cobham's blood and with a growing urge to impress the cause of civil aviation upon a largely indifferent administration, he decided to make an impact by delivering a petition to the government. This he did in 1926 by flying from Rochester to London, by way of Australia, landing on the River Thames in front of the Houses of Parliament before an estimated one million people thronging the bridges and embankments! His triumph was marred only by a freak incident which resulted in the death of his engineer and long time companion, Arthur Elliott. This occurred when a lone tribesman fired a shot at Cobham's aircraft flying low over the Euphrates river. The bullet entered the cabin and severely wounded Elliott who died in the RAF hospital at Basra the following day. Cobham was persuaded to continue the journey as a tribute to his friend, whose duties were taken over by Sergeant Ward, on loan from the RAF.

Alan Cobham was knighted immediately following his return to England and having become an international celebrity, found himself in great demand for public appearances throughout Britain and the United States. By now confident of his own resourcefulness and ability to support a growing family, he decided to branch out on his own. Leaving de Havilland in May 1927, he founded Alan Cobham Aviation Limited with offices in London's New Bond Street, which he shared with the notable racing car designer and driver Malcolm Campbell.

The opportunities for developing air travel in Africa had become obvious to Cobham during his Cape Town venture. At the same time, northern air pioneer Robert Blackburn was investigating similar possibilities and their joint interest led to a 22,000 mile route survey flight by Cobham in a Short Singapore loaned by the Air Ministry, and to the creation of Cobham-Blackburn Airlines in 1928. Cobham's ambitions to own his own airline were thwarted, however, when Imperial Airways decided to extend its routes into Africa, and Cobham-Blackburn Airlines was officially wound up in 1930. Nonetheless, Sir Alan was not quite finished with the 'Dark Continent', and in 1931 he departed on yet another route-proving expedition. Flying a Short Valetta equipped with the largest floats ever built, he carried out an extensive survey of the lakes and inland waterways of central Africa, and by so doing, achieved the unique distinction of having travelled across and around this immense land mass by conventional landplane, flying boat and seaplane!

Cobham's engineer Arthur Elliott and Sir Sefton Brancker flew to India and Burma in D.H.50, G-EBFO.

Although Jumbos are a common sight on today's airports, they were not so common in 1924! At Jalpaiguri, an elephant guard was mounted to prevent souvenir hunters damaging the aircraft.

At home in Buckland Crescent, NW3, the day after his return from India, Cobham recounts his adventures.

'FO, now fitted with a 385 hp Jaguar engine, receives energetic attention from Arthur Elliott at Stag Lane. Imperial Airways contributed £500 to ensure that any photographs taken of the aircraft en route to Cape Town showed the IA emblem.

Cobham, Elliott and cameraman
Emmott, just prior to departure for
Cape Town.

Off again! On 15 November 1925, family members including Cobham's wife, father and mother
(centre) and Emmott's brother and sister (left) braved the mists at Croydon.

The location is Luxor, and 'FO provides welcome shade for some of the local population.

'The Smoke That Thunders'. While circling low through the spray over Victoria Falls, water entered the Jaguar's carburettor. Imminent engine failure caused Cobham several anxious moments.

Sir Pierre van Ryneveld who, along with Sir Quintin Brand, made the first flight to South Africa in 1920, congratulates Elliott and Cobham at Pretoria.

A welcoming party of D.H.34 (top), H.P.W8b (rear centre) and D.H.9 aircraft escorts Cobham into Croydon.

Touchdown at Croydon on 13 March 1926.

On show at Gamages. A rather weary looking 'FO vies with the camera for the crowd's attention.

Re-equipped as a floatplane, 'FO, its crew and sponsor, Sir Charles Wakefield, pose for the camera at Short's Rochester works before the flight to Australia.

A final fill up on 30 June 1926, and one of the last pictures taken of Elliott before his untimely end.

The Royal Air Force provided the burial party for Elliott at Basra.

He's arrived! Cobham circles Essendon aerodrome at Melbourne, at the end of the outbound journey on 15 August 1926.

This bird's eye view shows 'FO on the ground in front of the hangars.

The strong arm of the law is strained by the crowd determined to glimpse the new arrival.

The thin police cordon soon gave way and people, apparently oblivious to the whirling propeller, close in on Cobham's aircraft.

Stand well clear - please! The white police horse appears to be the only spectator not wearing a hat.

Gladys Cobham receives news of her husband's safe arrival in Melbourne.

Son Geoffrey and family friend *Major* keep in touch with events.

Meanwhile back in Australia - Cobham and replacement engineer Arthur Ward are accorded a hero's welcome. Here Cobham, in the centre of the second row, appears about to succumb to fatigue. Ward is just behind Cobham's right shoulder. Note the RAF 'wings' sported by the ladies of the revue.

Sleeping sickness grips theatre crowd! Although Cobham and Ward might be forgiven for nodding off in the left hand box, others in the audience also seem to be 'more than relaxed'.

Britain's premier pioneer pays his respects to Australia's own Ross and Keith Smith, who were the first to attempt the flight to their homeland in 1919.

To shrieks from ships' sirens and the roar from a million people lining the embankments and bridges, Cobham sweeps in over Westminster Bridge.

To a population still attuned to horse and cart transport, Cobham's 26,000 mile round trip using the same airframe and engine was a breathtaking achievement.

Standing room only! Note the adventurous souls on top of the GLC building chimney stacks.

Journey's end! It is 2.26 pm on 1 October 1926, and a sweet moment for Cobham as he touches down on the Thames.

Cobham is transported to the steps leading to the terrace of the Houses of Parliament by watermen of the Port of London Authority - whose average age might be just a little more than that of today's employees.

Worth waiting for - Mrs Cobham
claims lost husband.

Alan Cobham explains to a mixed gathering that includes King Abdulla, the Minister for Air
Sir Samuel Hoare, (behind the table), and Crown Prince Hirohito, that there was 'nothing to it
really'. Mrs Cobham appears to have caught the dreaded Australian sleeping sickness disease.

'And the nominees for the 1926 Tailor and Cutters' Guild Fashion Award are: Capel (Armstrong Siddeley engineer) Cobham and Ward'.

Not under arrest but accompanying Mr Whitley, the Speaker of the House at Westminster.

Alan Cobham was awarded the Air Force Cross and made a Knight Commander of the British Empire immediately after his Australian exploit.

Steady as she goes! Sir Alan directs the unloading of a D.H.Moth (and Lady Cobham) from the deck of the SS *Homeric* in New York at the start of a combined sales and lecture tour.

City slickers! Sir Alan and a heavily pregnant Lady Cobham pose in Toronto during the 1926 lecture tour.

A new venture. Africa again, this time with Lady Cobham in the crew and serious route planning in progress.

With a Short Singapore I G-EBUP loaned by the Air Ministry, and the backing of Sir Charles Wakefield, Cobham and a crew of five set off on a 22,000 mile, six month journey around Africa on 17 November 1927. From left to right: C.E. Conway (engineer), Capt H.V. Worrall (co-pilot), Lady Cobham (secretary/cook), Sir Alan Cobham, F. Green (engineer), S.R. Bonnett (cinematographer).

Up and away; the Singapore leaves the Medway at Rochester.

At Malta Lady Cobham was presented with two canaries which also made the historic voyage around Africa.

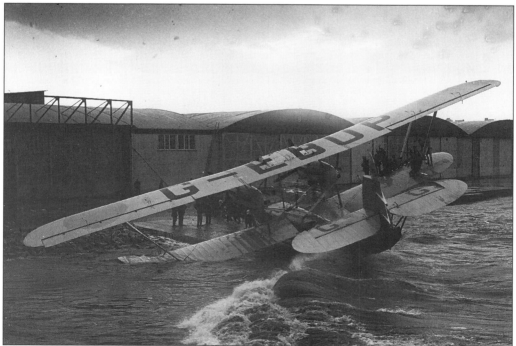

Storms at Malta resulted in severe damage to the Singapore and an eight week delay.

Administration - African style.

Running repairs and overhaul on G-EBUP, the first flying boat to visit Durban in March 1928.

It is 31 May 1928, and home at last. Lady Cobham hands luggage to RAF attendants at Plymouth.

A west country welcome for the Cobhams at Plymouth.

The Cobham's younger son Michael does not seem enthralled to be greeted by a rather fearsome looking Captain Worrall.

Immediately following their return from Africa, the aerial adventurers undertook a 2,000 mile journey around Britain's seaports. Shown here on arrival at Newcastle, are the Cobhams with Capt H.V. Worrall on Lady Cobham's left, and Brigadier P.R.C. Green, Secretary of the British Air League, on her right.

A wet and windy finish to the tour. The flying boat crew are received by the Mayor of Rochester, Councillor F.C.A. Matthews, but the smiles for the camera, perhaps unsurprisingly, seem a little forced.

This 1928 advertisement for the Ingersoll Watch Company displays little of the sophistication used by today's marketeers.

ALAN COBHAM AVIATION LTD
150 NEW BOND STREET
LONDON W.1.

DIRECTORS.
SIR ALAN COBHAM K.B.E.
Lt COL WARWICK WRIGHT D.S.O.
~ E.A.MERCKEL ~

MAYFAIR 2904
~ GRAMS ~
TALSUNDAR LONDON

11th July, 1928.

E.S. Daniells, Esq.,
   Managing Director,
   Ingersoll Watch Company, Ltd.,
      Ingersoll House,
         KINGSWAY. W.C.2.

Dear Sir,

The story you have heard about our INGERSOLL watch is quite true.

On the evening before we left Southampton, at the commencement of the Sir Charles Wakefield Flight of Survey Round Africa, I smashed my wrist watch for the third time.

It was essential that I should have a reliable timepiece so I decided to purchase one that evening. It was just on closing time when I noticed a little shop which was displaying INGERSOLL Watches; I entered and bought one of your famous Crown Watches, which the girl handed to me together with the usual guarantee.

On our first day's trip in the Short Rolls-Royce Flying-Boat I accidentally dropped the Watch, breaking the glass, and therefore had to hang it up in the cabin by a piece of string.

It was of the utmost importance for us to have an accurate timepiece because it was by time alone that we could estimate our fuel consumption and the length of time we could remain in the air without landing. Readings had to be taken every half-hour of all temperature gauges and other instruments.

I discovered that all our time records were being taken from the INGERSOLL with the broken glass, as none of the other watches on board could be relied upon, and for seven months, throughout the 23,000 miles of Survey Round Africa, with all sorts of varying climatic conditions, the INGERSOLL acted as our trustworthy timepiece.

It now occupies a prominent position in our office, and continues to function perfectly.

Yours very truly,

Alan J. Cobham

Cobham's final long distance aerial survey flight to Lake Kivu in Central Africa, took place in 1931. Here he inspects the Bristol Jupiter XI engine installation in the Short Valetta seaplane. Note the four bladed propeller construction.

Initial launch of the Valetta. The workforce provide a sense of scale that shows the massive size of the 40 ft metal floats.

Cobham lifts off the Medway on his five week 12,000 mile survey flight on 22 July 1931. Upon its return G-AAJY was evaluated as a landplane, before finally being scrapped in 1934.

Family separations - and reunions - were all part of the flying business. Younger son Michael is seen here on the left, beside brother Geoffrey.

Four

Cobham Comes to Town

As the 1920s progressed, Cobham's desire to carry the cause of civil aviation to officialdom and the general public blossomed into a crusade, and by 1929 he had assembled a small team of administration and technical staff to support an intensive Municipal Aerodrome Campaign tour of 110 towns and cities within the British Isles. Flying a D.H.61 ten-seat machine purchased from de Havilland, he embarked on a twenty-one week campaign during which he carried approximately 40,000 passengers and made some 5,000 landings. His typically strenuous routine usually involved arrival at the new location by mid-morning to provide flights for local officials - an opportunity Cobham invariably used to promote his services as an aerodrome consultant and to pinpoint the advantages an airport would bring to the area. The post-lunch period was devoted to free flights for school children, and the rest of the day to earning revenue from flights for the general public.

Upon completion of the tour, it was decided to employ the D.H.61 on a special Imperial Airways route survey programme in Southern Rhodesia and accordingly, Cobham safely delivered the aircraft to the survey party in Salisbury without mishap. However, on his arrival in Cape Town prior to travelling home by sea, he was dismayed to learn that it had crashed during take-off. Fortunately there was no loss of life but the aircraft was completely destroyed.

By 1932, Cobham's enthusiasm had turned towards providing a touring airshow. Although formally registered as National Aviation Day (later Display) Limited, his travelling fleet of aircraft and airborne performers was more popularly referred to as 'Cobham's Flying Circus'. Skilled aerobatic pilots, wingwalkers, parachutists and novelty turns thrilled crowds the length and breadth of the country, and also, during the winter of 1932/33, at locations throughout South Africa.

It was estimated that over 3,000,000 people paid to see the shows and that perhaps as many - scathingly referred to by Cobham as 'hedge guests' or the 'Aberdeen Grandstand' - viewed the events gratis from nearby vantage points! Well over 1,000,000 people enjoyed their first flight with the 'Flying Circus', and although many flying organisations undertook barnstorming tours throughout the 1920s and early '30s, none achieved the success and lasting fame enjoyed by Cobham's highly professional team.

The tours ended in 1935 as Sir Alan Cobham began to experiment once more with setting up a small airline. Cobham Air Routes operated briefly between Croydon, Portsmouth, Bournemouth and Guernsey, but after the loss of an aircraft and its pilot, the fledgling airline was sold to Olley Air Service Ltd.

Cobham purchased this D.H.61, G-AEEV, which he christened *Youth of Britain*, from de Havillands for £3,750. Following his Municipal Aerodrome Campaign tour, he sold it to Imperial Airways for £3,000.

The twenty-one week tour was highly successful and Cobham lost no opportunity to impress public and officials alike that 'aviation had arrived'.

Cobham's 1929 tour arrangements were placed in the hands of General Manager Dallas Eskell, third from right. Between Eskell and Lady Cobham is Sir Charles Wakefield, who provided free flights for 10,000 school children.

Cobham surveys a map showing his ambitious tour itinerary for 1929.

Dallas Eskell, on the extreme left, helps to manoeuvre the D.H.61 into position.

Michael and Geoffrey Cobham await their father's less than elegant arrival!

Cobham, after delivering the
D.H.61 to Southern Rhodesia for
Imperial Airways, met his family
and returned by sea. Seen here
after their arrival in England, the
hunting rifle strikes an
incongruous note.

Magnificent machinery! Sir Alan, on one of his many public engagements, inspects Mrs Roger's
1929 MG18 at the Concourse D'Elegance rally, Eastbourne, 1930.

Sir Alan and Lady Cobham with
Captain A. Ward, who was
responsible for Alan Cobham
Aviation's publicity campaigns. The
group are seen at Mrs Stanley
Baldwin's flying rally at Hanworth
Air Park in 1930.

The boss! - along with an immaculate public announcement van and purposeful looking
Blackburn Lincock.

The 'Circus' formation *en route* to yet another destination. Left to right: Avro 504, Tiger Moth, Handley Page Clive, Fox Moth, Spartan MKII (nearest camera), Avro 504 and (below) Cierva C.19.

Dagenham, 14 April 1934, and the 'Circus' gets under way for the first show of the season. The Airspeed Ferry prepares for take-off as the Handley Page Clive gains the crowd's immediate attention.

Cobham addresses local dignitaries at Sutton, Cambridgeshire, on 12 September 1934, in a scene repeated on hundreds of similar occasions throughout the country. The Airspeed Ferry awaits customers in the background.

Cobham's long association with Aerofilms Ltd continued throughout the National Aviation Day Display years.

Part of the large fleet of vehicles that accompanied the 'Flying Circus' tours. The long container in the forefront transported Joan Meakin's glider.

Cobham, who availed himself of this D.H.9 for his personal use during the summer tours, is seen here at Lower Hall Farm, Walthamstow, in April 1932.

The touring team pose in front of the Handley Page Clive. The flying personnel are sporting Royal Flying Corps' style uniform.

Geoffrey Tyson picks up a handkerchief with a wing-tip-mounted prong. Flying a Tiger Moth, he performed this piece of precision flying at over 800 'Flying Circus' airshows.

This Handley Page W10, one of two used for passenger joy-riding, is refuelling Cobham's Airspeed Courier prior to his unsuccessful non-stop flight to India in September 1934. G-EBMR later crashed at Aston Clinton, near Aylesbury, killing four crew members.

At airshows in the 1930s public car parking was not the problem that it is today.

Wing-walker Martin Hearn demonstrating his 'hands off' approach on top of an Avro 504.

Part of the Grand Fly Past that always opened the airshow. The Airspeed Ferry leads, flanked by D.H. Moths, an Avro 504K and two Dessoutter monoplanes.

Flying legends; Alan Cobham poses with fellow long-distance aviator Jim Mollison in front of a Tiger Moth.

Accidents did happen. A mid-air collision over Blackpool on 7 September 1935 resulted in the crash of this Avro 504. The pilot and two passengers were killed, but the other aircraft involved, a Westland Wessex, managed to land safely.

Ringmaster *extraordinaire*! Kenneth Aitkin's delightful caricature of Sir Alan Cobham was featured in the January 1992 edition of *Aeroplane Monthly* magazine.

Handbill distributed at Staines, 8 October 1933. Whether the public was reassured to know that the pilots' fitness routine was sponsored by a brewery is undetermined.

The winter of 1932/33 saw a scaled down version of the airshow performed at seventy-seven locations in South Africa. The Cobham family are being welcomed home by Captain Ward.

Cobham acted as technical adviser for several films associated with aviation. Here the message may well be 'Good luck my boy - but we don't expect you to come back'. The roles of the other gentlemen remain obscure.

It looks as if he made it after all! The intrepid stunt man being rescued from the Welsh Harp, near Hendon.

Cobham Air Routes was not a success and was taken over by Captain G.P. Olley after only three months in operation.

Five

The Vital Link

By 1935, times were changing and Cobham, realising that the public had become sated with airshows, decided to sell his organisation to C.W.A. Scott, in order to concentrate on the development of aerial refuelling; increasing an aircraft's range and payload were problems that had exercised him frequently during his earlier long distance flights. In order to keep his core team together in the winter months following his airshow tours, he experimented by passing fuel from one aircraft to another using a trailing hose. This method was not new and had been employed to refuel many aircraft attempting endurance record flights, particularly in the USA during the 1920s. Cobham, however, was determined to introduce a system that would be suitable for commercial use and to this end, on 29 October 1934, he registered a new company, Flight Refuelling Limited. Firstly with Imperial Airways and later the Asiatic Petroleum Company (Shell) as major shareholders, and with aircraft loaned by the Air Ministry, he embarked on trials that led to the successful non-stop crossing of the Atlantic by mail-carrying Short 'C' Class flying boats in August 1939. Although no practical use was made of air-to-air refuelling during the Second World War, by 1948, Flight Refuelling's equipment was being used by the United States Air Force.

In the late 1950s and early '60s, the company's 'probe and drogue' method of aerial refuelling became a mainstay of Royal Air Force and Royal Navy operations following its earlier adoption by the United States Navy and Marine Corps. Today, employing either (or both) the British 'probe and drogue' method or the American 'boom' system introduced by Boeing, the transfer of fuel in flight - the vital link as foreseen by Sir Alan Cobham - is a commonplace feature undertaken by major air forces throughout the world.

Since its formation, Flight Refuelling has engaged in many diverse activities. During the Second World War it carried out research and development on behalf of the Royal Aircraft Establishment and its tanker aircraft also played a crucial role in the Berlin Airlift during 1948-49.

The company's enforced move in 1948, from Ford aerodrome in Sussex to Tarrant Rushton in Dorset, coincided with an increase in manufacturing operations. As the '50s progressed these assumed greater importance than the company's flying activities and necessitated the construction of a new factory at Wimborne. Various flying programmes continued at Tarrant Rushton however, until the airfield closed in 1981, after which they transferred to Bournemouth International Airport. Initially undertaken by Flight Refuelling's Airfield Division, the Cobham organisation's wide range of flying duties are now conducted by FR Aviation Limited.

How prophetic! A cartoon reproduced from a 1909 edition of Punch magazine.

The Ford Motor Company operated its Trimotor aircraft from Ford Aerodrome, named after the nearby village. Cobham's Flying Circus and pre-war refuelling development teams were also based there until 1940. After spending the wartime years at Malvern and Staverton, Flight Refuelling returned to Ford before finally transferring its operations to Tarrant Rushton.

Cobham and Sqn Ldr Bill Helmore (right) attempted a flight-refuelled non-stop flight to India in September 1934.

It was after Cobham's Airspeed Courier had refuelled from this Malta-based Handley Page W10 tanker that a failed throttle linkage caused the flight to be abandoned.

Using aircraft loaned by the Air Ministry, Cobham conducted aerial refuelling experiments over the south coast. The 'nose-to-tail' method required the operator in the tail turret of the leading Vickers Virginia to catch the trailing hose with a walking stick!

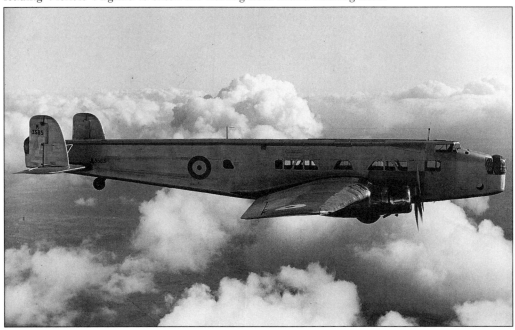

Another tanker used was the Armstrong Whitworth AW23, forerunner of the Whitley bomber.

The Solent, 1939. Pre-war trials culminated in Flight Refuelling's Handley Page Harrow tankers assisting mail-carrying Short 'C' class flying boats to cross the Atlantic non-stop.

Harrow tankers were stationed at Gander in Newfoundland, to support the transatlantic trials.

Refuelling trials were also undertaken at the Royal Aircraft Establishment (RAE) at Farnborough until all development work was transferred to Flight Refuelling in 1938. Here a Westland Wallace is refuelling a Hawker Hart during RAE trials.

A Boulton Paul Overstrand, on the left, is in contact with a Vickers B19/27 during tests at the RAE.

Ford became a front line Fleet Air Arm station in 1940 and Flight Refuelling moved to the Morgan Motor Works in Malvern, taking over the six bays on the left of the main entrance.

Following a short spell at RAF Defford, Cobham's flight test department moved to three new hangars erected at Staverton. Shown here is a photograph taken in 1986 of Bellman hangar SE2, used by Flight Refuelling during the Second World War.

One project undertaken at Staverton involved the towing of Spitfire and Hurricane fighters by the Wellington shown here.

After each aircraft had taken off under its own power, but with the tow rope connected, the fighter's engine was shut down and the bridle tow released.

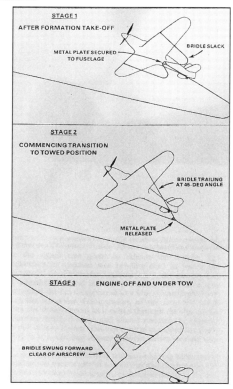

STAGE 1
AFTER FORMATION TAKE-OFF

METAL PLATE SECURED TO FUSELAGE

BRIDLE SLACK

STAGE 2
COMMENCING TRANSITION TO TOWED POSITION

BRIDLE TRAILING AT 45-DEG ANGLE

METAL PLATE RELEASED

STAGE 3   ENGINE-OFF AND UNDER TOW

BRIDLE SWUNG FORWARD CLEAR OF AIRSCREW

The release sequence, although shown to be feasible, was not adopted for service use.

In addition to de-icing programmes involving several types of bomber, Flight Refuelling crews flew this Halifax Mk III, NA684, to determine the detonation characteristics of various fuels for the Shell Petroleum Company during 1945.

Although no longer taking an active part in Sir Alan's business activities, Lady Cobham (centre of back row) was very much involved with war work organisations such as the Malvern Women's Voluntary Services.

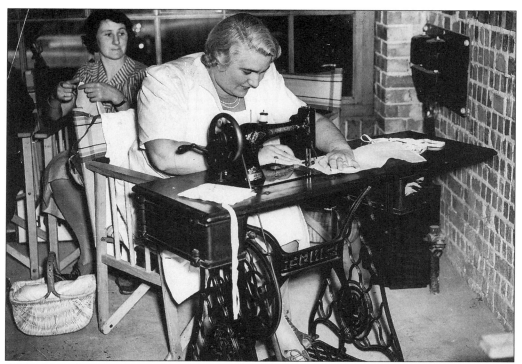

All hands welcome!

In 1946, Flight Refuelling returned to Ford where it continued aerial refuelling development with a fleet of Lancasters, two of which gave a demonstration at the SBAC Flying Display held that year at Radlett. G-AHJU and G-AHJT are on the front row.

A converted Lancaster G-AHJV flown by ex-RAF Pathfinder chief Don Bennett made the first non-stop refuelled flight from Heathrow to Bermuda in May 1947.

Flight Refuelling's Chief Engineer C.H. Latimer-Needham (on lower step), with Don Bennett and Sir Alan Cobham, after the aircraft's return to London.

The Lancaster tanker installation showing grapnel and hose nozzle.

The 'looped hose method', used pre-war and immediately post-war, required the pronged grapnel with attached steel cable to be fired from the tanker across a weighted cable extended from the receiver. With the cables thus enmeshed, it was possible to draw the fuel hose down into a mating receptacle.

Flight Refuelling's technical representative Bill Woodus, with the Greener Gun used to fire the grapnel.

The company conducted refuelling trials over the Channel (1946), the South Atlantic (1947) and North Atlantic (1948) with British South American Airways and British Overseas Airways Corporation crews. Although the trials were deemed technically successful, the arrival of bigger aircraft with more powerful engines meant that refuelling systems were never adopted by civilian airlines.

This BOAC Liberator was used as a receiver during the North Atlantic trials.

The relocation of the company to Tarrant Rushton in 1948 coincided with the start of the Berlin Airlift. Here seven of the company's fleet of thirteen tankers are ready for the next sortie at Fuhlsbuttel.

Coke and hot dogs were typical fare for the crew whilst their aircraft was unloaded.

This aircraft crashed on 22 November 1948 with the loss of seven Flight Refuelling personnel *en route* to Tarrant Rushton.

At the peak of the airlift, 652 personnel were engaged at Tarrant Rushton on the continuous repair, overhaul and maintenance of its tanker fleet.

Flight Refuelling's 'looped-hose' equipment enabled this USAF B50A *Lucky Lady II* to complete a record round the world non-stop flight in 94 hours in March 1949.

Tarrant Rushton airfield was used by Flight Refuelling from 1948 to 1981, although manufacturing and administration personnel moved to other local premises in the early 1960s.

Using the newly invented 'probe and drogue' method of refuelling, Flight Refuelling's test pilot, Pat Hornidge, set up a 12 hour endurance record flight in a Gloster Meteor MK III. Ten refuellings were carried out from the converted Lancaster tanker.

The modified Lancaster tanker, showing the refuelling operator's vantage point.

Two Lancasters had their nose sections reconfigured to provide the pilot with better forward visibility and were entered as G-33-1 and G-33-2 on the civil register.

The refuelling probe installation on the endurance flight Meteor EE.397.

The USAF sent B.29s and F.84s to Tarrant Rushton for conversion to 'probe and drogue' tankers and receivers in 1950.

A B29 receiver engages with a KB29T tanker during the conversion flight trials.

The company's last piston-engined tanker was Avro Lincoln RA657, shown here about to supply an F84 Thunderjet.

The first use of air-to-air refuelling in a combat zone was over Korea. Here a KB29T passes fuel to a Lockheed P-80 Shooting Star in July 1951. Note the refuelling probes mounted on each wing tank.

Cobham visited the USA to promote his company on many occasions. Pictured with him in July 1948, is long-time colleague Percy Allison, in the centre, whose innovative ideas were reflected in many refuelling equipment patents.

The drawing office at Tarrant Rushton in the 1950s.

The parachute store, shown here in 1953, was another wartime building converted for company use.

The early 1950s saw Bristol Brigands undergoing conversion to the T4 trainer role.

Stored at Tarrant Rushton were several ex-BSAA Avro Tudors, which Cobham at one time considered purchasing in order to set up an air freight charter company. The Tudor was also considered as a potential tanker for the de Havilland Comet.

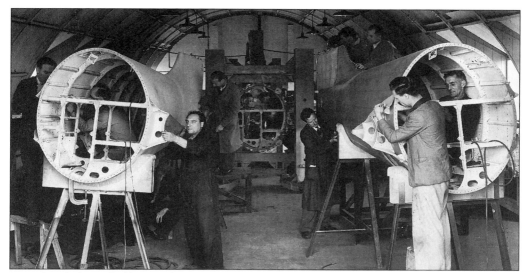

In 1952, Flight Refuelling took over a sub-contract to manufacture 415 Sea Hawk rear fuselage units for Armstrong Whitworth. The airframe construction shop appears to be very heavily populated!

Some 650 Meteors of various Marks were repaired and overhauled at Tarrant Rushton for the RAF and other foreign air forces. In addition, the RAF's No. 210 Advanced Flying School was the only jet training unit serviced by a civilian company. Part of the AFS's establishment of thirty-six Meteors, Vampires and a sole Airspeed Oxford are shown here.

As many as 119 Meteor MK 4s and 92 Meteor MK 8s were also converted to become U. MK 15s and U.MK 16s for use as unmanned drone targets. The photograph shows a number of U.Mk 16s at Tarrant Rushton.

Two D.H. Mosquito MK XIX's, G-ALGU and G-ALGV, were purchased by the company for air charter work, but were disposed of soon afterwards.

Throughout the 1960s Flight Refuelling enjoyed a close association with the Belgian Air Force and many F-84F Thunderstreaks, shown here, and T 33 Shooting Stars underwent Inspection and Repair programmes in the Tarrant Rushton hangars.

In 1959 Michael Cobham, who had joined the company seven years previously as a non-executive director, went to the City to further his higher management and industrial experience, returning as deputy managing director and chief executive in 1961.

A meeting of old hands! Sir Geoffrey de Havilland and Sir Alan Cobham at Hatfield in September 1960.

Meteor TT20s were used initially to evaluate towed target systems produced by Flight Refuelling, under licence from the American Hayes Corporation.

Flight Refuelling's own highly successful Rushton winch and target system was developed on Canberra TT18 aircraft.

Test flying of the company's MK20 refuelling pod, developed in the late 1950s for the Royal Navy's Scimitars and Sea Vixens, was test flown on this Canberra B2.

The talented executive team at Tarrant Rushton. Mike Goodlife, extreme left, led the company's design team and Peter Macgregor, third from left, provided the inventive inspiration for the 'probe and drogue' refuelling and Rushton winch systems. Also shown are, (from the left): Peter Procter (Sales), Sir Alan Cobham, 'Harry' Harrison (Engineering), Chris Tonge (Finance), Edward Rossiter (Publicity) and John Pochin (Administration).

To meet the company's growing needs a new factory was constructed at nearby Wimborne in the early 1960s.

Sir Alan's choice of rose bushes was made after much discussion with expert nurseryman Harry Wheatcroft.

Flight Refuelling achieved its major breakthrough with air-to-air refuelling when the RAF formed its first dedicated tanker unit, No. 214 Squadron, equipped with Valiants in 1958. The Lightning shown here was a particularly thirsty fighter.

Victors took over from the Valiants in 1964 and became the backbone of the RAF's tanker fleet for thirty years. No. 50 Squadron's Vulcans also served as 'stopgap' tankers in Europe when the Victors were transferred to Ascension Island during the Falklands War in 1982.

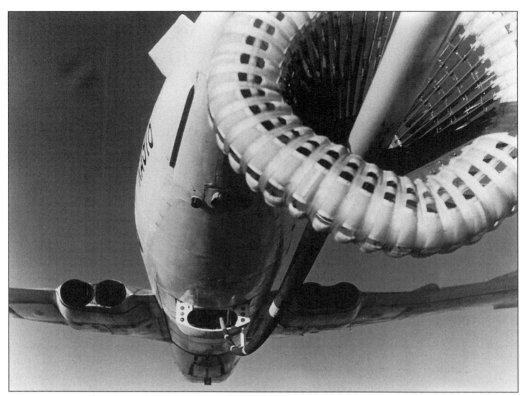

A Victor providing refreshment from its MK 17B hose drum unit.

A Phantom being fuelled from the MK 20C wing pod of a Royal Navy Buccaneer.

All trailing! This pleasing study shows to advantage the Victor's wing and fuselage-mounted refuelling units.

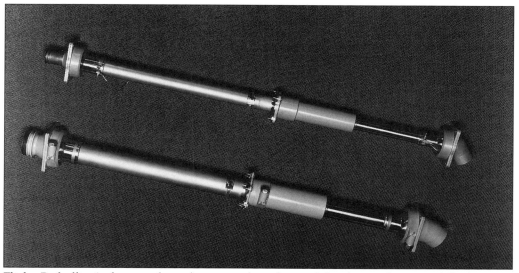

Flight Refuelling's fortunes have been greatly influenced by the production of fluid system components for aircraft throughout the world. Illustrated above are the telescopic fuel and air joints fitted in the swing-wings of the Tornado.

Following the company's successful Meteor drone conversion programme, a small number of Sea Vixens was also modified to become the D.MK 3 variant. This aircraft is shown at what is now Bournemouth International Airport, following the transfer of company flying activities in 1980.

The year is 1981: the end of an era at Tarrant Rushton.

The range of unmanned flying vehicles produced by Flight Refuelling includes the Falconet subsonic target (above) and the Phoenix artillery reconnaissance aircraft. Both are currently in production for the British Army.

Large scale items such as this 2,250 litre fuel drop tank fitted to the Tornado, required a special facility to be built at the Wimborne factory.

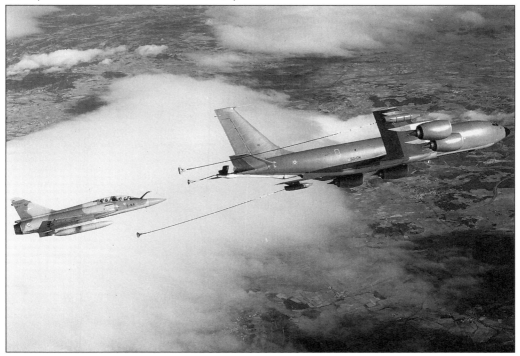

Flight Refuelling's latest refuelling pod variant, the MK 32B, is fitted to many tankers throughout the world, including the French Air Force C-135FR shown here.

Six
On the Lighter Side

'It's a full time job being Alan Cobham!' the man himself once remarked, and this visual scan across the years has surely shown some, though certainly not all, the reasons why.

Possessed of enormous energy and enthusiasm for whatever life had to offer, he indulged his love of horse riding and sailing whenever possible and paid meticulous attention to the planning and maintenance of his large and beautiful gardens. His appreciation of the arts lay principally in music, and he was for many years closely associated with the Western Orchestral Society. Demand for his attendance at public functions, usually as guest of honour, was ceaseless, and his role of director of several companies in addition to his own gave him a grasp of local and international affairs second to none.

The steadying influence in his frequently turbulent life was Lady Cobham who, by calming his more extreme ambitions, always sought to maintain a normal family life. That she succeeded so well may be deduced from many of the images shown in this book. Sir Alan was devastated by her death in 1961 and for years thereafter devoted his time exclusively to the planning of the new factory in Wimborne. In 1969, in his seventy-fifth year, he finally relinquished the reins and handed over the role of chairman to his son, Michael, who, by then, was also managing director.

After a spell of well earned retirement in the British Virgin Islands, he returned to England and died on 21 October 1973.

What more could a man want? A flying picnic - 1920s style.

Sir Alan and Mr H.G. Young, Manager of the Odeon Cinema, Littlehampton, cut debonair figures at this 1939 appeal for RAF recruits.

Family fun in Switzerland with sons Geoffrey, left, and Michael, just prior to the Second World War.

Westwinds, Middleton-on-sea, the Cobham home near Ford, during the late 1930s.

At Tarrant Rushton, Sir Alan, assisted by welfare officer Mary Lewis, prepares a mountain of Christmas presents for employees' children.

During the 1950s, the annual Children's Day at the airfield was always eagerly attended.

The celebration of Flight Refuelling's twenty-first birthday took place at the Bournemouth Pavilion in 1955.

Off the Dorset coast - a sailor's life for me!

One of the last pictures to be taken of Lady Cobham at The Willows, in Tarrant Rushton village.

The Willows; close by is Tarrant Rushton churchyard, where Sir Alan and Lady Cobham are buried.

THE MAGAZINE OF THE WESTERN ORCHESTRAL SOCIETY BOURNEMOUTH

THE WINTER
GARDENS SOCIETY
Magazine

Howard Coster

SIR ALAN COBHAM K.B.E., A.F.C.
Chairman of the Western Orchestral Society Ltd.

No. 23   Price One Shilling   Winter, 1956

Patron of the arts.

ALAN JOHN
COBHAM
1894–1973

Under Michael Cobham's
chairmanship the organisation
expanded to form, in 1982, the
FR Group plc. This in turn
became Cobham plc in 1995.

Sir Alan enjoyed visiting his
customers and is seen above, on
HMS *Hermes* in 1966 and below,
signing the distinguished guest
book at RAF Little Rissington
the same year.

Near the end of a life's work, Sir Alan formally opened Flight Refuelling's sports and social club on 4 September 1971.

Knighted upon his retirement in 1995 as Chairman, Sir Michael Cobham is now President of Cobham plc.

Sir Michael Knight succeeded Sir Michael
Cobham as Chairman of Cobham plc in 1995.

Guiding the Cobham group toward the
Millenium is Chief Executive Officer Gordon
Page.

Seven

Flying into the Future

More than sixty years have elapsed since Sir Alan Cobham founded Flight Refuelling Limited. From that early beginning an organisation has evolved that embraces many other major, subsidiary and joint venture companies which also supply equipment and services to the aerospace and defence industries.

It has not been the intention here to dwell on these associated companies that now contribute so much to Cobham plc's success and corporate identity. What these pages have attempted to unfold for the reader are the flying-related adventures which, although set in motion so long ago, provided the basic building blocks for the group that today still proudly carries the Cobham name in the international market place.

FR Aviation operates a fleet of over twenty Falcon 20 aircraft for electronic warfare and threat simulation training. The Company's main bases are at Bournemouth and Teeside airports

The Dornier 228 is FR Aviation's chosen vehicle for carrying out coastline patrol duties.

The last of thirteen VC 10s converted to the C MK 1 (K) tanker configuration by Flight Refuelling and FR Aviation, was delivered to the RAF's No. 10 Squadron on 6 February 1997.

Canberras are no strangers to Bournemouth and a life extension programme on the RAF's PR 9s was completed in 1995.

Extending the Cobham flying legacy is the Nimrod 2000 assembly programme at FR Aviation that will produce the RAF's Maritime Reconnaissance Patrol Aircraft for well into the next century.

Major Nimrod assemblies are, individually, delivered to Bournemouth in the Antonov 124 heavy-lift transport.